The Vagaries of the Heart

The Vagaries of the Heart

by

Desmond Childs

First published 2024 by The Hedgehog Poetry Press,

5 Coppack House, Churchill Avenue, Clevedon. BS21 6QW

www.hedgehogpress.co.uk

ISBN: 978-1-916830-22-6

Cover Design © Micheala Childs   www.maycontainglitter.com

Contents

To my daughters Micheala and Elizabeth

for all their help and encouragement

VERITIES GOWN

Through graven eyes,
peers the chivalry of love
Verities gown; to adorn your desire
Oft held, in reach of fervors fleeting glance That discreetness; be perceived
by silence taut upon the lips and ears of many Though desire was not
spoken, but held within the virtue of true love Cleaved to, adored within
the beat of hearts impassioned embrace Veracity though; be a beast with
woes In revelation, renunciation Now Ajar, this most closed door of
courtly love

FRACTURE

The petals unfold
the breaking bloom of
hairline cracks in fragile glass
the ringing tone - singing
of friction pressed upon the lip
of silence
speechless words unspoken
moving eyes - stare back
a multitude of gazes
fractured - the crisp sound crack
of shattering glass

YIELD

The thought was traceable
Back to your heart
As you yield
your love and flesh to me
Your grace, with passion,
In our desire of
flesh on flesh
I give my soul to you
For we shall yield together

WE'LL MEET AGAIN

Even as the passion spoke
in the warmth of love
of that last embrace
She knew his words
where lovers lies
Spoken for comfort
in their last goodbye
Her thoughts they run
to a distant shore
Where death awaited
and his last thoughts lie
But remembered is
that last embrace
As only she, remembers now
How dead men leave
their grief in harts

STONE

this was the eleventh hour
cool words upon your breath
the nights chill spoken
edged with; stones cold caress
no ember flickered
no last minute redemption
the twelfth hour struck
with the hand of the guillotine

JIG

with her tune, she bound me
her melody, from deep within
she played the tune, subdued me
with her violin
she wrapped heart strings around me
and brought me to my knees
she pulled my soul before me
with her fingers deftly ease
she drew the bow and slew me
I dance a deathly jig
to the tune, that she plays me
upon her violin

ABOUT DESMOND CHILDS

Born in Birmingham, Desmond now resides in Lichfield with his family and two dogs. He is a dedicated outdoorsman who works for the local Authority. He spends much of his leisure time tending to his garden, where he likes to grow various fruits and other produce. Desmond's poetry draws from real-life experiences and the complexities of human relationships, with an added element of fantasy. His work has been featured in anthologies by Hedgehog Press, and his poem Bedlam won, A Bestiary of Night.

"Vagaries of the Heart" is his first standalone publication.